City Witch

THE CITY WITCH COLLECTION

by
Christopher Penczak

**COPPER
CAULDRON**
PUBLISHING

Credits

Writing: Christopher Penczak
Proofreading: Sharon Morrison, Justin Gaudet
Cover Art & Design: Steve Kenson
Layout & Publishing: Steve Kenson

Acknowledgements

Thank you to the spirits of the cities of Boston, Cambridge, and New York, who inspired my exploration into urban practices. Thank you to the staff of Fort Apache who put up with my weirdness for three years. It was an amazing, fun, albeit short ride. Thank you to the staff of *new Witch* magazine, particularly Anne Niven and Dagonet Dewar. And thank you to Steve Kenson and Adam Sartwell, for encouraging me to release these article as an anthology.

Disclaimer

This book and all spells, rituals, formulas and advice in it are not substitutes for professional medical advice. Please confer with a medical professional before using any herbs, remedies or teas in any manner. Unless specifically indicated, formulas are not intended to be consumed or ingested. The publisher and author are not responsible for the use of this material.

Copper Cauldron Publishing does not endorse any suppliers or resources mentioned by contributors.

For more information visit:

www.templeofwitchcraft.org
www.coppercauldronpublishing.com

ISBN 978-1-940755-00-7, First Printing

Printed in the U.S.A.

TABLE OF CONTENTS

INTRODUCTION

The world that spawned *City Magick* feels like it was from another lifetime and, in some ways, it was. I describe my life then as a previous incarnation, before being reborn into the life I currently have and could never have dreamed about then. But, like all past lives, our current one is built upon the foundations we have laid out in our past, and it can be beneficial to review how we got to where we are now.

One of my formative magickal experiences was using my magick in everyday situations, and these uses shaped some of my unorthodox practices. When I began my path as a Witch and magician, I was in college, in the run-down mill town of Lowell, Massachusetts. While it has gotten a refurbishment since, at the time the hunt for non-dangerous commuter parking and surviving the incredible winter cold when waiting for a shuttle was one of the main reasons for using my magick. My intentions were purely practical. I was studying music business, and forays from Lowell into Boston to see bands and meet people were frequent.

Soon I found myself working in Cambridge, Massachusetts, the sister city to Boston across the Charles River, and less involved with my teachers, coven, and studies in magick. I practiced a very personal and eclectic form of Witchcraft with close friends, and had the unique challenge of keeping my nature-based Sabbat and Esbat, solar and lunar, practice going, while working long hours in the city. I found myself sneaking magick into my breaks, and between dinner and whatever show I was attending.

When I found myself ejected from that world due to company lay-offs, my journals from the time formed the nucleus of my first published book, *City Magick*. Up until that point, I did not see myself as a particularly urban practitioner and, when my career as a teacher, tarot reader and, ultimately, author took off, I found myself relocated back to the more suburban New Hampshire town where I grew up. Today, I still don't necessarily see myself as deeply entwined with the urban experience, but the Universe had a new curve ball for me.

I was asked by the editors of a then-new magazine called *new Witch* to write a regular column called "City Witch." The magazine's tag line was "not your mother's broomstick" emphasizing a fresh, young, and modern approach to the Craft, balancing the publisher, BBI Media's, other publications like *PanGaia* magazine. I foolishly said yes, even though I was concerned that I said all I had to say in my book.

My life then took off in a different direction. I had not anticipated the subtle intricacies of life as a metaphysical author. I was soon asked to travel to promote my work. In these days, publishers still arranged author book-signing tours and industry trade shows. Soon, I got invitations to speak at Pagan festivals and conferences, and then offers to teach weekend intensives at various stores and centers. I began a crazy, semi-nomadic life as the modern day "man in black" moving from town to town, sharing magick and connecting people who would not otherwise gather together.

The travel brought me to a number of cities I had never visited before, or had never visited after my magickal training. I again had the struggle of maintaining a spiritual practice outside of my normal locale, without my usual tools and peers for support. Each trip brought new inspiration, new ideas, and a new way of looking at the world of magick while out in the world. These became the seeds for my *City Witch* column. Soon my column was right there with other talented writers and teachers, such as Phil Brucato, Galina Krasskova, Jason Pitzl-Waters, Tasha Halpert, LaSara Firefox, and editor and author, Dagonet Dewr.

Several years passed, and my goals and focus changed. My ideas for a new column for young Pagan leaders clashed with vision and direction of the powers that be at *newWitch* and I stopped writing articles and focused even more on my books and teaching. Eventually I was asked to be on the cover of *newWitch* with a feature story on my work before it discontinued publication to merge with *PanGaia* as *Witches & Pagans* magazine.

My first publisher, Red Wheel/Weiser decided to repackage *City Magick* around its ten year anniversary. Though given a new cover, new introduction, and new foreword by respected Witchcraft author and dear friend Judika Illes, they did not want to include any new material in the book. I had envisioned either working the concepts of these articles into the main text, or using them as an appendix for a new generation of urban magicians. Sadly that was not to be the case, though I adore the new cover with a mix of old world magick and new urban qualities to it. The original cover had a picture of New York's twin towers, and in a post 9-11 world, it was always a bit odd to display that book on the shelves.

No matter where I traveled when teachings and doing book signings, someone would bring an old copy of *newWitch* to me to sign, or talk about how an idea in one of the "City Witch" articles helped them look at magick in a new light. So with some encouragement from my partners, we decided to gather the original articles together for a new anthology, *City Witchcraft*.

Ironically, I had an initial dispute with my publishers, who wanted to change the name of *City Magick* to *City Witchcraft* right before publication. They feared it could be mistaken for a book extolling the virtues of urban living, and not get shelved with the other metaphysical, New Age, and magickal books. I objected since it was primarily about the practice of magick and shamanism, not necessarily the religion of Witchcraft. We compromised with a spelling of magick with a K, as Aleister Crowley popularized, to differentiate it from any other form of magic. I soon found myself altering all my writings to embrace the spelling in my first book to be consistent, and consequently delving much deeper into the world of Aleister Crowley as a result. His teachings of Thelema have certainly influenced my views on magick.

As years have passed, I've certainly looked at my Craft as not only a religion, but a spiritual vocation, broadening my definition and function of the word Witch. I have no problem calling this *City Witchcraft,* for it helped teach me how to function as a Witch in an urban environment and on the road. It is my hope that the articles continue to provide inspiration in working magick everywhere you are, for everywhere is sacred and magickal. You simply need to open your eyes, ears and heart to the magick all around you.

Blessed be,
Christopher Penczak
Lammas 2013

CHAPTER ONE:
LOCATION!
LOCATION!
LOCATION!

Location is everything. It doesn't matter if you are choosing a home, picking a school, or doing sacred work. Each location is a pocket of potential energy, and that energy will influence all that you do. The ancient practitioners of magick knew this, and their sacred sites of power become arenas of mystery to the modern world. The powers of the Giza Pyramids, Stonehenge, and the Serpent Mound are sought by modern practitioners looking into the mysteries. But in seeking out power in only the places of old, we do not find the magickal energy all around us.

In my experience, every location is a vortex of energy, including the urban environment. Cities are built because they are founded on such powerful swirling pools of energy. This energy is one of the things that attract settlers, even if most only feel the pull intuitively. As each city develops, it gains its own flair, personality and psychic "climate". It develops a relationship with the people inhabiting it. Not only does each city gain a "vibe" all its own, each section of the city, each district and neighborhood, develops its own energy.

The gift, and the challenge of the modern city Witch, is to partner with these vast energies. In the paradigm shift to a holistic model of life, we cannot disown the structures and societies we have created. Most would agree that modern city life is not perfect. Far from it. Many Neopagans would have us run to the woods, and that's fine. I enjoy the woods and I've lived and worked in rural environments, but they are not the only places to find and work magick. Nor should they be. Magick is needed even more in the urban jungle. Through acknowledging these energies, we can heal, transform and honor all locations as sacred space. But if we never see the magick in these places, we will never partner with it.

All locations have an energetic signature. The impressions we get by visiting these locations become symbolic interpretations of the energy of the area. Magick is working through a symbol system to create change in your world. Most symbol systems are based on ancient alphabets, arcane rituals and esoteric teachings, but ultimately they are just symbols, from the Qabalah to sympathetic magick, and once they are understood, they can be applied.

Locations hold the same information too. The financial district appears to be high energy, often tense or exciting as fortunes are made and lost. It is a symbol of that high energy of risk, power and prosperity. Other systems may use the symbol of the Wheel of Fortune card in the Tarot or the planets of Mars and Jupiter. The little neighborhoods of the *avant garde* artists and musicians symbolize the creative pursuit, the drive to express and communicate through word, song, shape and color. Astrologically, the planets of Venus and Mercury might represent these forces. In rune magick these creative urges may be expressed through the runes Kenaz and Ansuz. An herbal magician might tap into these energies using Lemon Verbana, Scullcap, or Almonds. The choices of correspondence are often personal and vary amongst different traditions, teachings and practitioners.

Here is a system to use locations in your own city or home town to create magickal symbols. In some ways this system mimics the sigils of high magick's planetary squares, but with a modern twist. I can only give you examples, you will have to create your own symbols based on the energies where you live and work.

Below is a map of Boston's subway system and various trains. By connecting points on the map that correspond to my intentions, I have created magickal subway symbols that I've drawn on a piece of paper or wood. I carry the symbol with me as an amulet or talisman of power. You can do the same based on maps of the subways and streets of your own town.

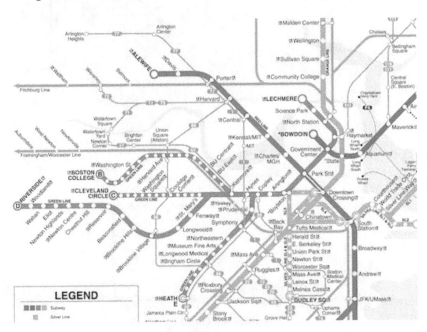

Part of the Boston MBTA or "T" subway system

This is the basic layout of all the main subway lines in the Boston/Cambridge area. To me, the arrangement of lines has always looked magickal, like an old glyph from some dusty tome of magick. But you can work with specific points on the map to create other symbols.

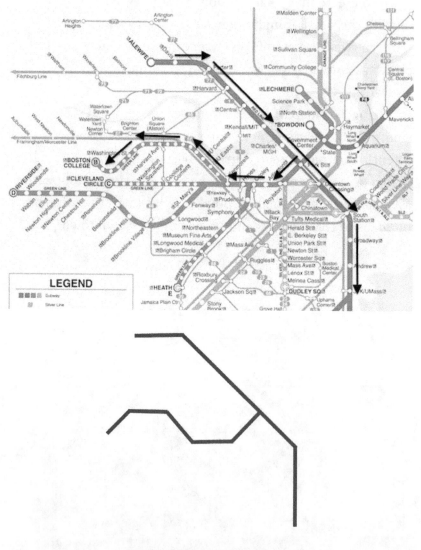

Symbol for Good Grades

City Witchcraft

With the intention of creating a symbol for good grades in school, you can pick points on the subway map that represent learning and education, such as the schools Tufts University, Harvard University, M.I.T., Boston College, and the University of Massachusetts. By connecting them via the already established subway lines, you create a magickal symbol for learning and good grades.

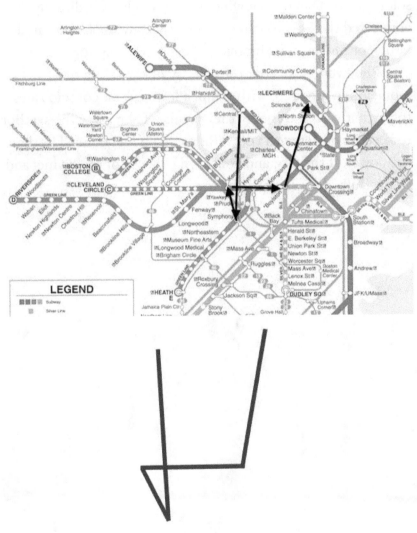

Symbol for Creativity

By tapping into the areas known for the arts and creative vibrancy, you can create a talismans to invoke those energies in your life. Here I've chosen Central Square, a spot of many clubs and local bands, the Theater District, Kenmore Square, another musical hip spot, and Symphony Hall. Lastly I chose Science Park, the location of the Museum of Science, because sometimes science must be the most creative art in devising its solutions. Instead of following the subway lines, I directly connected the dots to make my creativity symbol. You can do either, or mix both techniques. The choice is up to you.

When you make your own city symbols, take a few moments to meditate with them, allowing your consciousness to partner with the energy they invoke. Then carry the symbol to keep its power with you. When you no longer need it, thank the power of the city, and your own concept of the divine, and respectfully dispose of the charm.

CHAPTER TWO: VISITING THE CELESTIAL CITY

Urban magick. City shamans. Both conjure the image of the literal concrete jungle and we seek to find the magickal in our surroundings, often despite their man-made appearance. Cities are not natural. Cities are not magickal. Cities are not sacred. It is because of these claims I wrote my first book, *City Magick: Urban Rituals, Spells and Shamanism*. Even in embracing the city and seeing the sacred wherever you are, it can still feel as if you are looking for the sacred under a rock. As modern Pagans, Witches, shamans and mages, we have been fairly conditioned to long for this epic past of perfection, a technology free utopia, a garden of paradise. Witches look to the supposedly matriarchal Stone Age cultures claiming a perfect paradise without violence, war, crime or any social ills. Even in the most rose-colored views of the ancient past, one must admit that such societies had their own challenges and problems.

Only in the truly mythic world do we see the perfect utopia. And mythic cities abound in our ancient Pagan mythology. If we look to the old stories for guidance and inspiration for the modern practices of Paganism, how can we claim cities are not magickal? The archetype of the city is the home of the gods themselves! When we have created real cities, we have been laboring in the shadow of the divine kingdoms. We think the concept of the urban Pagan is a modern one, coming long after our industrial revolution and modern technology, but there have always been forms of urban magick. The first ancient cities of Sumeria, Egypt, and Chaldea were full of magick. Many of our magickal, artistic and philosophical ideas come from the cities of Greece and Rome. Witches and wise ones, herbalists, and midwives were in many villages and cities when they could survive. Magick is wherever life is, in any form. So magick has been ever present in cities, even when we didn't recognize it.

Stories of cities, halls, and temples in the other worlds abound in world mythology. We have Asgard, the home of the Norse gods, where the divine halls of Odin and Freya are home to the spirits of fallen heroes. We have the mountain home of the gods of Olympus, the Greek pantheon. In Celtic mythology, we have the four mythic cities Falias, Gorias, Finias, and Murias, symbolic of the four sacred directions, and the four gifts of the Tuatha de Dannan, the children of the goddess Danu, who carried the Stone, Spear, Sword, and Cauldron. In the East, we have the fabled ascended cities, filled with spiritual masters, places like Shamballa or Shangri-La.

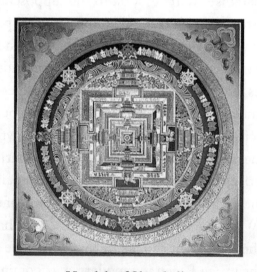

Mandala of Shamballa

Shamanic practitioners report vast cities in the upper worlds, made of glass, crystal, amber or even light itself. These sky realms are populated with beings that dispense wisdom and advice, but often lack the fierce challenges of the underworld journeys. The heavenly castles and shamanic kingdoms have devolved into our fairy tale stories of climbing the beanstalk and finding a castle in the clouds. They become the heavenly bliss promised to us by many religions.

In the shamanic model of reality, with the middle world or mortal realm, underworld, and upper world, the concept of cities, writing, and even what we now call civilization is really part of the upper world domain. The lower world is the primal jungle, the forest, the place of trials, testing and power. Many consider the underworld earthier and goddess oriented. Few cities exist in the primal dwellings of the underworld. Perhaps in our modern Pagan effort to get in touch with this previously neglected aspect, we have exclusively focused on its archetypes, excluding things like cities.

The upper world, on the other hand, contains the aspects we have focused on. Often less challenging or fearsome than the lower world, many choose to focus on the heavenly realm exclusively. The sky realm is more linear, more logical, less emotional, and more directly intuitive through the power of knowing, rather than interpreting psychic visions and images. In the sky realm, beings often tell you things directly, while the underworld beings make you figure it out for yourself. I think that is one of the reasons when we swung, historically, toward prominence with the sky and warrior gods, city building was a natural extension of it. If the shamans of the Stone Age experienced cities in their upper world vision, they must have seemed mythic and otherworldly. Such buildings were unattainable. But only through their divine vision, only through the magickal imagination could humanity get such ideas. And only in the age of the sky gods could such an attempt to bring the heavens down to earth be attempted. But in the end, our middle world creations are only a pale reflection of the heavenly ideals. They are the shadows to the divine city and, as such, reflect it with the problems of modern cities. Issues such as overcrowding, pollution, noise, politics, crime and economics are found in both ancient and modern cities.

To heal our relationship with modern life, and come closer to manifesting some of the ideals of the higher realms, without losing sight of the lessons and wisdom of the underworld, we can reconnect to our own personal version of the celestial city. Use this guided imagery to help create your own journey to the ideal urban city of light.

Journey to the City

Begin by preparing yourself for the journey. Light any candles and incense that help you find that meditative state. Purify the room with any banishing rituals you use, or simply imagine filling the room with a crystal white light to purify and protect. Turn on any meditative or drumming music and choose a comfortable position.

Close your eyes and imagine yourself in your favorite city. It can be where you live, or someplace you haven't seen in a while. Imagine yourself walking down its streets, walking to a place of personal power. You will know it when you find it. Keep walking until you come to the heart of your urban sacred site. It could be a particular building in the city. Often it is a place with or near a tall building.

Imagine this building as your magickal ladder, your world tree or axis mundi. This is the world scrapper, the building that connects all realms, all lands. Its foundation is in the underworld; the peak is in the heavenly upper world. Before you enter, a magickal being may appear to you, a city totem animal, or urban spirit. This is your guide to the next level. Follow your guide if that feels right to you.

Enter the building, and find your way to the top either by the stairs or elevator. Continue your pattern, climbing, endlessly climbing, higher and higher. Make your way higher and higher up to the heavenly realm. Be lost in the pattern of your movement, all the sounds your journey makes.

Like Jack and the Beanstalk, you emerge at the top into a cloud filled panorama. You emerge into the heavenly realm. You can walk in this wispy air, which becomes more and more solid with each step. You feel a path draw and call to you.

In the distance you see the celestial city, made of glass and crystal, light and sound. Go towards it, taking notice of all that you see along the way on this celestial roadway.

Enter the gates of the celestial city and feel yourself fill with light. You take on the qualities of the upper world as you enter. Explore this city, finding its places of power and speaking with the guides and beings of the upper world. Ask how you can bring this wisdom back down to the Earth.

When your visit is complete, take this time to thank the Celestial City and its inhabitants, and follow your paths back through the clouds, back down through the building and center yourself back in your place of power. Bring your awareness back to the body, and ground yourself as needed.

Use the energy of the Celestial City to transform your ideas of the sacred and bring the highest ideals into the material world. Only through making everything and everywhere sacred will we truly heal the world and transform our society.

CHAPTER THREE: CALLING THE URBAN GODS

One of the traditional means of communicating with the ancient Pagan gods was through communion with the land. As many deities were described as having intimate links to the natural land, if not the full embodiment of it, the land served as a interface for sacred communion.

Both mystics and everyday Pagans took advantage of this. One need not be initiated into the ancient mysteries to take an offering to the river. Working with the land was simple, intuitive and accessible to everyone. We know of, and now modern Pagans imitate, traditions involving pouring a libation of wine out to the earth during ritual. Some do it out of tradition because that's the way they learned it. Some do it as a sign of reverence and respect. Others do it because they know everything has energy. That wine, or any offering, has not only inherent energy, but energy invested in it by you, the magickal practitioner, through your intention, prayer, or ritual. The offering itself acts as medium to carry your energy.

The combined energy is used to build a bridge between our human consciousness and the consciousness of those power beings we call the gods. Though divinity is manifest everywhere around us, it takes our conscious perception of it, bringing our awareness to it, and the intention to communicate, to build a relationship with these beings. Once the link is established, and developed over time, it's like having a more direct connection to divinity. Certain practitioners of magick relate well to a particular god or goddess naturally, due to temperament, symbolism, and past life associations. If they put the time into building that relationship, other psychically sensitive people can't help but notice the connection. It becomes a part of your every day life. You live in a greater partnership.

Places of particular importance are where the "worlds" meet. Offerings are traditionally brought to those places that are liminal, points between that are neither one nor the other, where gateways are created between the worlds, letting us commune more easily with the realm of the gods. Where water and land meets is such an in-between place. Oceans and rivers are places where offerings are made, though they can sometimes be very different offerings. The ocean can be used to cleanse and remove, to purify. Many Witches use ocean water as their salt water, to bless the altar and add to potions. Fresh moving water brings blessings back to you. Stagnant water is used to bind, curse, or make contact with the underworld beings. Anything that runs deep in the land has an underworld connection. Our custom of throwing a penny down a wishing well is a remnant of making an offering to the gods of the depths. Likewise, a spring relates the healing and regenerative waters rising from the depths to use in the world of mortals. Caves hold the initiatory power of the underworld. Burial grounds allow us to commune with the ancestors. Mountain tops, where land reaches to sky, are important sacred spaces. Here we talk to the loftiest of divinities, the sky and stellar beings. Magnificently large trees bridge the underworld, middle world, and sky realm, forming the basic image of the shaman's world tree.

So what happens when you don't have a local well, bog, or mountain top? Many of these natural practices have fallen out of popularity, and not reclaimed by many Pagans because of their urban environments. Many urban magicians focus on the work where one can close the door and be undisturbed in a bedroom or living room, rather than go outside where people will see them. And even if they did go outside, where would they go?

Others, I'm happy to say, ignore all those worries. They take the spirit of the traditions and adapt them to their current environment, taking great inspiration from the African Diasporic traditions living in the same urban environments and doing quite well. Traditions such as Voodoo, Santeria, and Ifa have not only embraced their urban homes, but found ways to thrive in them. Local rivers, crossroads, graveyards, statues, and sewers become foci for their rituals.

Building a Bridge to the Underworld

Since a recent trip to England and speaking with European Pagans and magicians, and some more traditional craft friends, I've been fascinated with curse tablets favored by the Greco-Roman culture. Much like a petition spell, but often carved on lead or wax. They ask the gods for retribution against one who steals or has wronged the author. Though there were many forms of cursing tablets and variations thereof, my favorites were the ones thrown into wells, bogs, and caverns. The tablets were like a letter to the gods. The lead corresponds with the concept of curses and the underworld sphere.

Today, I don't have a lot of lead tablets just sitting around, nor places to throw them. I'm not terribly fond of doing curses, but I just love the concept of these little tablets. I work with the underworld gods a lot, and though that the urban environment, despite its solid asphalt streets, has a big connection to the underworld – the foundations, piping, subways – they are all very chthonic.

Though we lack wells, we do have storm drains, leading down into the underworld. I've had really great results writing my intention for a spell petitioning the dark underworld goddess, and wrapping it around a stone, small enough to fit through the grate, yet large enough to have a little weight to it. I tied the paper with a black thread, doing a bit of cord magick binding my intention to manifest as a tie it together. I've sprinkled some herbs into the paper first, making the whole thing a charm. Patchouli and mugwort are good underworld herbs, and easy to find. I make my journey to the storm drain a sacred pilgrimage, not following a linear route, but a round about circular one. Once the storm drain is at my feet, I hold my intention in my mind, repeat my petition under my breath and toss the package into the drain, letting go of it, physically and energetically, so it may reach the gods of the depths and manifest as a reality in my life.

Another underworld technique I like is used for healing. When one is injured or ill, a replica of the injured or diseased body part is made as a votive offering. Though most of us think of a votive as a type of candle, a "votive" is anything offered in devotion. Carved limbs or organs were offered to the gods, with the idea that they would consume the illness and return health to the organs. I love using clay in magick. You can use the same technique, molding an offering appropriate for your situation and casting it into the underworld storm drain as an offering for healing magick.

The underworld pokes out into the urban environment in other ways. Graveyards are my favorite, since the Northeast is rife with old ones. Many cities have graveyards, be they modern or historic. Offerings to connect with the ancestors can be made there. You might ask what the purpose is to visit such graveyards if your ancestors aren't buried there, but in the otherworldly view, all graveyards are one graveyard. All are beyond the bounds of normal space. All connect to the same underworld of the ancestors. All are portals and accessible if you use them with respect.

Walking the Middle World

The middle world, the waking world of mortals is also the world of the crossroads, where the world above meets the world below. The crossroads deities and guides open the gateways to otherworlds from this middle world. They stand besides us and show us the way. In the space in between space, all things are possible. You are able to align with the worlds and draw the things you want, or banish the things that no longer serve you, with the resources of all three worlds at your disposal.

One of the most important sacred sites in the ancient urban world was where roads intersected, but it's a crossroad of three paths, forming the "Y" shape or a crossing of two roads, forming four potential directions in the "X" shape. Our urban environment is filled with such crossroads.

One of the first acts of magick I learned before diving too deeply into the Craft was from a wonderful lesbian couple who lived in the urban confines of Cambridge, Massachusetts. The two were having some financial difficulties, and wanted a blessing of prosperity, yet wanted to maintain their artistic vocations. They baked a cake, filled with all the wonderful things that they enjoyed. They used spices that they loved, particularly cinnamon. The important thing is that it was something pleasing to them, and what they enjoyed in life. In correspondence magick, sugars are associated with Venus, and attracting what you desire, while spices such as cinnamon, are in harmony with Jupiter, and increased abundance.

The couple cut the cake into three pieces. On the third piece, they placed four coins. They went to the crossroad at the town square closest to their apartment, and dropped the cake in the middle of the square, as an offering to the crossroads gods. Then went home and each ate their 3rd of the cake, linking themselves to the offering they gave. Within a month, each had new business opportunities that substantially increased their income, yet was in alignment with their chosen artistic careers.

Prosperity magick is not the only workings of the middle world. I do more crossroads work asking for guidance, to the knowledge and wisdom to decide before embarking on a new path.

Upper World Offerings

The upperworld is classically associated with guidance, enlightenment, benign blessings from on high, rather than the more material concerns of the middle world and underworlds. Upper world magick has the resonance of theurgy, petitioning the gods and aligning with the divine source, though some use their petitions and alignments for less than noble causes. When thinking about how the upper world was contacted nature sans a mountain top or cliff, I thought of the old temples of the ancient civilizations, from shrines to towers and ziggurats, reaching for the heavens. In temple worship, incense and other offerings would be burnt, with the idea that the smoke would take the worshipper's prayers to the heavens to be received by the gods of the sky.

Like offerings to the depths of the underworld to build an energetic bridge between you and the unseen forces, incense offerings can be a great way of establishing contact with the upper world forces.

Though we might not have the mountain top or towering temples, we do have quite a number of buildings reaching to the heavens. We don't need to be on the largest building to do our ritual. In essence, any building will do. Any lift in perspective brings us a bit closer to the upperworld. You can make your offering on the rooftop of your apartment building, or on the windowsill or fire escape. Though I enjoy the view from the towering skyscrapers with observation decks, it's hard to do full ritual there. You can do some internal mental magick, without ritual tools, but if you want to burn offerings or light candles, its better to find a place where you can comfortably do those things in relative safety and privacy. I participated in a full Moon ritual on a rooftop, with a cauldron of incense burning, and there was something striking about the thick incense rising up between the buildings, while no body below us really knew what we were up to. There was an energy and intensity, despite us not being technically earthed, or touching, the ground. The purpose of our ritual was to reach the stars, and it worked quite well.

When you want to commune with the forces of the upperworld, find a place that reaches to the sky, be it your bedroom window, or some rooftop. Even a hill in your city could work well. Decide what substances will be appropriate by consulting with a good herb or incense book. My default offerings are sage and frankincense, though I experiment with a lot of different herbs and resins. Light a self igniting charcoal and place it in a flameproof vessel. Hold your offering and think of your intention. What do you seek the upper world for? What do you need help with? What do you want divine aid to help you manifest? Clearly form your intention and bless the substance with your will and prayer. Sprinkle your offering over the charcoal. Feel the energy rise up to the heavens, where it will return to you, like water vapor returning as rainfall.

Use the suggestions as guide for establishing your own calls and signals to the deities all around you, using your own environment. Magick must grow and expand, so feel free to experiment and share what works for you with others.

CHAPTER FOUR: FINDING A CAVE

One of our strongest spiritual archetypes, from east to west, is the concept of a magickal retreat. For some it conjures the image of the yogic ashram, or camping on the mountain top. My favorite image is the shamanic cave, retreating to the womb of the Goddess reminiscent of the Himalayan sages in their "mountain cave" retreats. But as a city Witch, how you do you find the perfect mountain cave retreat? You can't if you have your heart set on the romantic image. But if you are flexible (and, if you are an urban Pagan, then I know you must be) I have a solution for you.

Not to long ago, I was blessed with several days alone in a hotel room. What I thought would be boring long weekend consisting of trying to entertain myself, watching TV and sleeping in, became a weekend of magickal exploration, ritual and self discovery.

The hotel can be a modern mountain, filled with many personal, private caves. Here we can retreat from the world, and take time to rejuvenate and revitalize. While traveling to the mountains may not be feasible for everyone when the need for a retreat strikes, the idea of taking a magickal evening or weekend, just for you, away from your normal environment isn't that far out of reach.

The purpose of the spiritual retreat is to disconnect from the mundane world, to see the magickal world running parallel in the physical and to commune with these forces to bring transformation. The techniques to achieve such communion are:

Isolation

First a retreat from the people you are most familiar with, those you see daily, or those who know you well and ground you in your expected persona. Sometimes just getting away to someplace where no one knows you can bring a refreshing sense of new awareness. Typically magickal isolation is from all human contact, and done in silence, to commune with nature without human interaction or communication, forcing you to commune through intent and intuition. When retreating in the city, losing all human contact may not be possible, or even necessary. Perhaps all you will need is the "do not disturb" sign on your door. With a personal vow and some will power, you can make a break from most modern technology, refraining from TV, radio—literally "unplugging"—and traditional transportation, keeping things as simple as possible.

City Witchcraft

Breaking Eating Patterns

Anything that breaks us out of our normal routines and patterns, including our food patterns, can serve as a wake up call. When we don't eat the same things, at the same time, we break preconceived expectations about ourselves. Traditionally spiritual retreats had special cleansing or detoxifying diets, or fasting. Your urban retreat can be an excellent time to research and experiment with new eating patterns. If you plan on fasting, be smart and research a healthy, safe option. I favor detoxifying fruit diets and juice fasts. They clear the mind, heart, and body to receive wisdom from the soul.

Prayer

Prayer is the heartfelt communication of your needs and feelings to the divine, a communication from the deepest core of your being, not just your mind. Most Witches I know shy away from the word prayer because of the Judeo-Christian context they seek to escape. Personally I don't feel the word is inherently bad for Pagans and Witches to use, when you understand the true meaning of prayer. It is connecting with the divine and communicating. When the prayer for a specific request is fulfilled, we say the prayer has been answered. To a Witch, that is the same as a spell manifesting. I often describe spell work as ritualized prayer to my non-Witch friends. In the Native American traditions, the concept of prayer is synonymous with worship, healing, and our western concepts of prayer and spells. Shamans pray to the plant or animal spirits for the blessing of healing or harvest. In essence, they are doing the same thing a Witch is doing through ritual and spells. So whatever your method of communication, taking the time to do it intensely, with sole focus, is the last mechanism of the spiritual retreat

The spiritual retreat into our urban hotel cave can be very effective with these three techniques in mind, modified to suit your current situation. I'm sure some purest will squawk that a hotel room is no substitute for a sacred mountain. I agree. But I also believe the sacred is everywhere, if you look hard enough, and all you really need is yourself. So if you can't go to the sacred mountain cave, then why not go to the sacred hotel cave? If you can get healing or insight, then how can it be a bad thing? Taking time to be mindful, to do magick, and to remember the sacredness is the most important thing, superseding any other rule or tradition.

There is a tendency to think, "I don't have to go anywhere. I can make my cave in my own home." For Witches who live with others, that can be a greater chore. For those who live alone, somewhat easier, but it doesn't break you out of your habits as easily as a new environment. Home working, in the "home cave" of a room with a locking door is wonderful for everyday work, but when the situation arises that you need extra magickal space to create your inner transformation, splurge a bit and get out of the house.

To truly work well in your urban cave, take time to plan your retreat and ask yourself these questions:

1) Why am I doing this?

Magick is most effective with a clear intent, so what is your intent? The motivation doesn't have to be grand and lofty. Are you simply needing to get away form the everyday world and recharge you psychic batteries? Or do you have a greater working you wish to tackle, and need some space, privacy, and focus? Traditional visionary retreats were often for guidance, not necessarily manifestation of will. People fast upon the mountaintop with training from indigenous teachers to answer life's great questions – "How can I heal? What is my purpose? How do I find and use my power wisely?" You could go to develop and deepen your relationship with a particular goddess, god, totem, or guide. Such ritual spaces are often created at life transition points, even if you have clear guidance, to make an appropriate mark and boundary, such as entering a new serious relationship, changing careers, or entering a new phase of life, such as adult or elderhood. All these are great motivations, but so is "What do I find when I slow down and take some time for me?" Sometimes simplicity is the best key.

2) How long will I need?

Determine the length of your retreat and stick to it. Plan ahead and reserve the appropriate accommodations. We have a tendency to want to extend our retreats, particularly if we don't find the answers our ego wants, in hopes of not having to face our responsibilities. We often tend to cut it short, and assume nothing will happen because we don't want to hear the answers in the first place. Setting a time boundary and sticking to it, you create a clear mechanism into and out of the ritual space. Traditional first quests are one night, second quests two nights, and so on, up to four nights, but these vision quests are most often accompanies by fasting. Elders would know when the time set was done, and send others out looking for you if you didn't come back at the appropriate time. I suggest letting a magickal friend know what you are up to and checking in with you when you plan to be back. Though there is little chance you will starve, freeze, or be eaten by wild animals in your hotel room, it never hurts to play it safe, particularly if you are working with powerful issues and energies that you have been avoiding.

3) What do I need to bring?

An important question indeed, since once you are there, you cannot go back to your home. You can, but you would be defeating the point of breaking contact with familiar settings. Gather only the essentials. For me, such retreats are more inner experiences, so the outer tools are less important, but I still like to have them. I might bring a basic altar set up that emphasizes my intent for the retreat. Keeping it simple, you could use just a single votive candle to be a meditative focus. Use whatever calls to you in designing the ritual. You can even make a quest for an appropriate altar item part of your retreat, as a sidewalking exercises. (For more on sidewalking meditations, see my book, City Magick: Urban Rituals, Spells and Shamanism.)

With these questions answered, you are ready. Once arriving at your hotel cave, make it appropriately suited to your work, arranging things in a pleasant manner for you.

I always do a banishing and protection ward in a new space, even if I am not doing a spiritual retreat. You have no idea who was here before you, so as the cleaning service empties it physically, it is up to you to clear it psychically. Since most hotels frown on sage and incense, particularly in non smoking rooms, I clear it by visualizing violet light. You can also use spray bottles filled with a solution of 50% water, 50% clear alcohol and a few drops of your favorite essential oils, creating a "smokeless smudge" spray.

Then I create a shield of prismatic crystal around the entire room, all walls and ceiling, including bathroom, to create a safe space, with the intention of barring all spirits and energies that do any harm.

If you are going to set up an altar, shrine, or meditative focus, do so now and dedicate it. I also dedicate it to my intent, by writing out the retreat intention on a piece of paper and keeping it on the altar. Then follow your guidance and traditions for going inward and creating sacred space. Your ritual retreat can involve formally casting a circle, doing dream magick, mindfully eating your meals, meditation, shamanic journey, or journaling. What technique will take your furthest in this moment? Perhaps a technique you don't have the time or space for in your everyday life. Take the time now. Create. Rejuvenate. Make magick in your sacred urban cave.

CHAPTER FIVE: Second Sight Seeing

Everything is magickal. Everything has the potential to show us the mysteries of the universe. We often think that magick only occurs in very neatly compartmentalized periods. "When I choose to meditate, do ritual, or attend a workshop, I am open to magick. Otherwise, I have a typical, ordinary everyday life." I used to think that way, but magick kept creeping in where I least expected it.

Travel has become one of the most mind-blowing experiences for me. Whether it is business or pleasure, the act of changing locations is very magickal. Changing your surroundings helps you change your consciousness. When I leave my everyday life and routines, my awareness widens. I think of so many rites of passages and initiation ceremonies that require the practitioner to leave the safety of the community and keep vigil in unfamiliar surroundings, such as a cave or mountaintop. When you think about it, so many gods of magick are also gods of travel. They are the deities of the inner journey and the outer journey. Hermes/Mercury immediately springs to mind. When you experience otherworlds, you "journey" into them, your perception moves to a new place, much like physically altering your position to change your perspective on something. When you look at a painting or photograph from a distance, you can see it differently than when you are up close. You get a sense of the bigger picture and true meaning. When we have distance from our daily life, we often gain a better perspective on it and can see the patterns we create. Perhaps that's why many shamans live apart from their village, maintaining a different perspective.

The first time I experienced the magick of travel was on a business trip to Los Angeles many years ago, and I thought I was going crazy, seeing and hearing things along my travels that no one else was experiencing. The experience changed my outlook, and I no longer expect to keep my spiritual experiences in neatly confined places and times. Lately I've been doing even more business travel, and have noticed some patterns that can help any magickal practitioner open to the magick of travel. If you are leaving the routines of your daily life behind, you can use the trip to expand your awareness. You might gain insights into your life, or simply know the magick of a new locale. You can look through your psychic eyes, with your second sight, to see what lies beneath the surface and partner with the magickal energy of the city or town your visit.

The Crossroads

Much of my own personal practice consists of working with various guardian and patron entities. Whenever we leave our home, we have many routes, many choices in our travels. I start with an offering and communication to the patrons of the crossroads. Much of my travel is by plane, and when waiting around for a connecting flight in an airport, I realized how much the airport itself is like the crossroads of reality, a cosmic hub where many souls gather. We cross paths with people, with energies we would never normally come in contact with. So now when I reach my crossroads – the airport, train station, or even threshold of my driveway – I call upon the guardian of the crossroads to guide me and protect me physically and spiritual on my travels. Personally I call upon an aspect of Hecate because I have built a relationship with her in other works. Other gods associated with travel and crossroads include the Greek Hermes and his Roman counterpart Mercury and the two-faced Roman god Janus. Minor spirits of the crossroads were called *Lares Compitales* in Roman culture. In African traditions, Legba is the opener of the way and guardian of the crossroads. In Japanese myth, *Chimata-No-Kami* fulfills this role. I even harken back to my Catholic roots. All the men in my family wear St. Christopher medals, as the patron saint of travel. I carry mine in a medicine bag, but take it out and wear it when I travel. Call upon the deity or spirit that you feel is most appropriate. With this blessing, I find that my travel time is not only smoother and more harmonious, but I synchronistically run into interesting people and we share important conversations. With the awareness of the crossroads, the awareness that anything can cross your path, I become more conscious of the trip as a magickal adventure.

St. Christopher Medal

The Spirit of the City

In some tribal lore, seekers will ask permission of the land spirit before entering a new territory. Intentions would be stated and offerings made. I know that when I go into the wilderness to gather herbs, I ask permission of the spirit of the forest and its guardians to enter. I leave an offering of water, a strand of hair, or even healing light energy before I enter. When I have asked permission, the paths become clear. I find whatever I am looking for and in general, things seem easier. When I have neglected to ask permission, I have more difficulties. I get lost. I trip and fall. I get cut by thorns and whacked with a branch. I can't find the plants that I seek.

Now I've learned to do the same whenever I go someplace different, particularly new cities. If I am traveling in by plane, train, or car, I take a few moments silently in my mind, using my inner magickal voice, to call upon the spirit of the city. I introduce myself and state my business. I ask for the permission and blessing of the city to enter and then I listen. Each city has a different voice, a different personality, at least in my inner ears. I get a sense of how I will relate to the city. The qualities are hard to put into words, and can change with the seasons, but they are distinct. Seattle had a very "green" voice when I visited. It was very primal and old sounding, yet welcoming. San Francisco has a more bell-like voice, otherworldly. New York is always strong and powerful, yet sometimes feels male, and sometimes feels female. I listen to make a connection, to know and feel the energy of the city. I will feel that same quality as I drive or walk its streets, and will let those feelings guide me. Usually I get lost easily in new cities, but since beginning this practice, I've noticed that my sense of direction and navigational intuition in a new city has greatly improved.

Local Spirits

As each location has an over arching spirit, a *genius loci,* there are many other entities connected to the land. Practitioners of shamanic and underworld traditions often note how the underworld itself, and the entities found in it, from the faery folk to the guardian spirits, look different in the practitioner's inner vision when they physically begin their ritual in a different location. The underworld of Los Angeles is different from the underworld of Boston. You can do the same things there, and seek the same magicks, but the flavor is different. Though many cultures have stories of magickal races that could be called the faery folk, the description can vary greatly from the Mediterranean, British Isles, and Americas.

Some locations just seem better for certain types of spiritual work. I suggest meditating in your new location. Expand your consciousness outward. I usually start in my hotel room, and feel my perception expand outward with each exhale, until I have a vague awareness of the entire city. I try to get a feel for its energy and how that energy interacts with me. I ask, how we can partner together? Then I ask for a local spirit guide. Find a way to communicate with this guide, through inner vision, inner voice, or even the pendulum. Through your communications with this guide and your regular spiritual guides, find out if you have any work to do in this location. Will it aid you in a new area? Or could you possibly aid it? Remember spirit work is a two way street. Sometimes we have to be of service as well.

While I was in New York, the city spirits showed me how to feel the flow of energy between buildings like currents. I learned to feel a level of subtle energy that I usually ignored. It helped guide me to different places that I wanted to visit, and I learned how to flow with, not against these energetic tides. In Seattle I learned to do a full Moon ritual without any tools by calling upon the plant spirits that surrounded me.

My spontaneous awakening in Los Angeles showed me that this city is a great place to confront your shadow side. As soon as our plane entered the air space, uncomfortable feelings came up for me. I felt almost nauseous, but knew it wasn't physical. When I had some time to meditate and sense the energy around me, I felt a lot of different things. First was the human consciousness of many broken dreams and difficult quests. There was such a longing. I, too, once had dreams of musical stardom, so it reflected a lot back on me. When I scanned the area, I felt like the earth energy grids around the city were wide open, facilitating a lot of spiritual contact, but there was not necessarily any filters to block out unwanted contact. I'm not sure if it is the natural state of things, or due to fault line stress or pollution, but it just felt very open to me. I now think this is why so many psychic and mediums find their way to the area. I just had difficulty screening it out. I felt the astral was very active and a feeling of being watched for much of my time there. Three nights in a row, I was visited by a spirit that appeared to be part man, part snake. Its messages forced me to confront a lot of repressed fears and angers. Since it was unbidden, I thought I was losing my mind. In this new setting, it seemed more real than most of my spirit contacts. I couldn't banish it using the traditional rituals and my usual guides said that I needed to experience this. Overall it was good, but frightening. Since then I've learned to consciously partner with new cities and new spirits, before they decide to simply show up.

Closing Rituals

Any good magickal experience has its boundaries carved out ritualistically. If you begin or invoke, you should end and close the connection. As I leave a city I thank the spirits I have worked with and say farewell. As I end my trip, I again thank the guardians of the crossroads. Even though I am returning to my "normal" life, the experience helps me see the magick in my day-to-day travels.

So while you travel, be open to the information, energy and insight of your location. Most likely your trip will have a purpose other than spiritual expansion. You don't have to turn your vacation into a mystical quest. Simply be conscious and respectful of the new energies around you. Follow your intuition and synchronous events. Open your awareness to energy patterns, auras, and general gut feelings. "Read" the energy of locations as you might read the energy of people or objects. With this greater awareness, you can appreciate the beauty of the world around you, no matter where you are, and sight see through magickal eyes.

CHAPTER SIX:
URBAN
WILDCRAFTING

A few years back, something happened to open my eyes to the world around me. I started to take notice of things that I never saw or felt before. I pride myself in sensing the subtle energies and recognizing the sacred in places were most people don't. That's what my book, *City Magick,* is all about, recognizing the magick and sacredness of urban environments. Most people overlook them, or think they are not magickal. Then I had an experience in woods and fields that opened me to a deeper level of the city.

My experience was taking an herbal apprenticeship at the Misty Meadows Herbal Center in Lee, NH. There's nothing really urban about Lee, though its not far from the city of Portsmouth. As a Witch, I had been working with herbs for many years. I love to make potions, oils, incense, and teas. I knew a lot about the magickal and spiritual uses of herbs from my training and my own research into the field. But I didn't know much about the medicinal, or at least my medicinal knowledge of herbs was scattered. I decided I wanted to get a solid foundation, and understand the more practical wisdom of the herbs, along with the mystical.

Part of our training was many walks in the woods and fields. For six months, one weekend a month, we lived on the farm, taking our classes and doing hands-on work. In the weeks between, we had to complete a set number of apprentice hours working in the shop, making products, wildcrafting, harvesting and, most importantly, doing plant identification.

Our teacher, Wendy Snow-Fogg, took us on weed walks and hikes through the forest and fields, pointing out both medicinal and magickal herbs. Most plants have both qualities. Plant ID was completely new to me. Though I had a lot of herbal knowledge, I was the typical urban/suburban Witch. I knew how to ID my herbs because that is what the label from the store said. I bought herbs in jars, in tiny packets from Witch shops, and the really exotic ones from mail order. Some I could identify through smell or taste, but most came in a package from a store. I didn't grow it. I didn't pick it. I didn't dry it. Someone else did. I didn't know where they really came from. Though they were usually fresh and carried vital life force in them, for magick or medicine, I was divorced from the living, growing essence of the plant world.

As we started our journey, Wendy told us that we would never be the same, that we would never look at the world in the same way. She was right. Though I was changed in many ways, one was the recognition of all the plants around me, from cultivated gardens to roadsides. I saw power plants and green allies wherever I went. Things I knew from childhood, but had no name for, were actually powerful medicines. I had been using them in magick, but never recognized them growing all around me.

We continued our journey by having a list of plants we needed to locate in the wild, identify and take a pressing for future reference. It wasn't just technical. True we did have our wild flower guides and pictorials to help us identify our species, but it was a spiritual process as well. We were encouraged to spend time with the plant. Be in its presence. Look at its

City Witchcraft

symbolism, the play of elements within it. Was it earthy and low to the ground, or fiery with bright colors, spikes, or a spicy taste? Not only could I identify them from the leaf, flower, or stem, but we also learned to feel their energy. It's subtle and intuitive, but powerful.

The truly unexpected part of the journey came later. Afterward I had the opportunity to travel to many new cities when promoting my books. I love to wander the neighborhoods and soak in the different flavors. I usually would pick up the "vibe" of the neighborhood and its people, but now something was different. The plants of the city were talking to me. I would feel a pull, and from the sidewalk would be growing what I would have thought was just a weed, but now I knew what it really was. Many magickal plants are considered "just weeds."

With my eyes open, I saw many plants just "hanging around" in the cracks of the road, in the gutters, in the tiny little plots of land, near bridges and highway underpasses. The places most of us think are dead and lifeless were bursting with not only green life, but some rather exotic and special forms of green life. Some were cultivated. Most were wild. Others were escapees from gardens through their seeds being scattered by wind or wildlife.

These plants anchored a magickal energy, a spirit medicine. Even if they were not recognized. Even if they were not taken internally, they brought a new vibration to the neighborhood they lived in. Wendy talked about how certain plants would show up in your life because you needed that energy. The plant world would anticipate the human world's needs and send its representatives to help. It works on both a large and small scale.

Wendy mentioned how, the summer before the 9-11 attack, St. John's Wort was more abundant, at least in our area, than ever. St. John's Wort is used spiritually and herbally for trauma and to bring a sense of light, hope, and protection. Most think of it as a mood lightener, but it has many blessings as a tincture, oil, flower essence, or magickal charm. When I was in need of protection magick, but tried to deny that their was a problem because I didn't want to acknowledge that someone would wish me harm, nightshade and yarrow suddenly sprung up in my garden. Both herbs are used in protection spells. Notice what herbs grow around you. We are attracted to plants we both like and need. They are attracted to us and will come, even if we are not aware of them.

Though most herbalists believe using herbs grown near you is best, the environment in most cities doesn't make taking herbal medicine from such urban plants the best action. I don't suggest consuming any of the herbs you find in the sidewalk cracks. But you can use the local herbs magickally, and quite effectively. By working with living plants, and picking your own leaf or flower, you get in touch with the living energies. Wild craft small amounts of it, so the plant may still thrive in the city, but you can add a leaf or two your own charms and mixtures.

You can sit down next to a plant and "tune into" it. Any magick done with that plant will be much more effective. Herbal Witches develop a relationship with their herbs and can make a small number of herbs do most needful things, from healing to magick.

So on my journey, as I walked the streets of various cities, from Los Angeles, San Francisco, and Seattle to Denver, Columbus and New York, I encountered these powerful plants that you might come across in your own city.

Black Eyed Susan: Black Eyed Susan is a cone flower with a dark center, the eye, and bright orange petals. Though medicinal its roots can be used in a similar way to Echinacea, and in healing magick to help the immune system, the true magick of Black Eyed Susan is in the shadow self. This flower helps us see what we deny. As a charm, it facilitates our entry into the underworld, and in working with the dark goddesses and gods.

Burdock: Burdock is known by its bur-covered seed capsules. They easily get caught in hair and clothes. I found some at the edge of an unkempt urban lawn. The signature of the seeds and the deep root is to get to the root of an issue. The spirit medicine of Burdock is used for endurance. It helps us to stick to things, even when times are tough. It helps us endure a situation, and get to the heart of our problems.

Cinquefoil: Cinquefoil is also known as five finger grass or witch grass because its leaves often have a five-pronged motif, with yellow five-petaled flowers. Cinquefoil is used to undo hexes and curses. It is also used to help others understand your point of view. I have steeped cinquefoil in olive oil, out in the sun for a month. Though it has no real aromatic scent, the magick is in the oil now. I anoint candles when having difficulties with other people, so we can all understand each other better.

Clover: Clover comes in many varieties. You will most likely see red or white clover. Traditionally clover is a symbol of good luck, known by the stories of four leaf clovers. Their rarity brings luck since most clovers are three leafed. Red clover is known as an herb of prosperity and money. Ruled by Jupiter, it brings expansion. White clover is not so much for material wealth, but spiritual wealth and understanding.

Dandelion: Dandelion is by far my favorite weed. The plant is one of transformation, going from yellow flower to fluffy white fuzz. The deep taproot gives it the folk name "Earthnail," since it can be used for grounding. Herbally it is a liver medicine, and spiritually the liver is the organ of anger, so Dandelion can be used to identify, release, and heal anger.

Hawkweed: Hawkweed looks like a smaller version of Dandelion on first inspection, but with a closer look, they are very different. The stem is more solid, the root is not as deep, and the leaves are different. Hawkweed is used for seeing things more clearly, like the sharp eyes of the hawk.

Loosestrife: Loosestrife or purple loosestrife is the bright magenta weed that springs up in wet areas, taking over roadsides and marshlands. You can find them by the side of the roads all over New England and they are considered an environmental hazard, choking out other life. I find it interesting that some herbalists use it for eye issues and the spirit medicine of Loosestrife is for chaos. No wonder it is springing up everywhere! We don't see the world clearly, and we have created so much chaos. It has to keep multiplying. Carry a charm of Loosestrife with you when you enter chaotic situations, or when you need to perceive things clearly.

Milkweed: Milkweed stems contain a milky white sap, giving it its name. The sap is traditionally used to remove warts, and because of that has an association with Witches. Spiritually milkweed is about nourishment, and can be used in mother goddess rituals. It is also popular in spells for weight loss, weight-gain, or developing a healthy sense of body image.

Nightshade: Nightshade is one of my favorite magickal plants. Related to the more deadly Belladonna, Nightshade is an herb traditionally used in flying ointments to aid shamanic journey and astral travel. It's also used for protection and breaking hexes. You can use it safely and effective by drying it out and carrying it in a herbal pouch.

Pussy Willow: Pussy Willow has fuzzy catkins in the spring, giving it a soft, furry quality. Willows in general are special to goddess work, and psychic ability, I have found that Pussy Willow in particular is powerful in issues related to touch. Healing rituals for those who have been harmed or abused can use Pussy Willow to help receive a sense of safety in the realm of touch and physical contact with others.

Queen Anne's Lace: Also known as Wild Carrot, Queen Anne's Lace has a deep taproot, like a carrot, with a beautiful white lacey flower at the top. In the center of the flower is a black/dark red dot, said to be where Queen Anne was decapitated. It is also vaguely reminiscent of an eye. Queen Anne's Lace is used to expand psychic ability, opening the third eye, yet keeping you grounded and rooted to the physical world as well. It's a great charm to carry when you read cards or do other psychic work.

Yarrow: Yarrow is a guardian plant, showing up at the edges and boundaries of gardens and roadsides. Traditional herbal magick gives Venus rulership and it is used in love spells, though some modern herbal Witches share its dominion with Mars, since herbally it works on the blood and spiritually it protects us by healing holes in the aura and giving us a healthy sense of boundaries.

If you are not familiar with plant identification, get a good plant ID book with color photos for your geographical area. Have it on you as you walk not only field and forest, but sidewalk and alleyway. Learn about the plants all around you and see how your relationship with the urban green world transforms.

For more information on the Misty Meadows Herbal Center, visit www.mistymeadows.org.

CHAPTER SEVEN: MAGIC OF THE MODERN CHARIOT

In a previous life, I was a part of the music industry and, while I had done little jaunts here and there in a tour bus, my first book tour was my first serious "road trip" where I drove. In fact, it was the first major road trip I took completely alone. I started in a rental car in Seattle and made my way down the West Coast to San Diego over the course of twenty days, trying to visit every metaphysical shop I could along the way.

It was there, in the confines of my little rental car, that I realized road trips are a modern form of initiation. Not the formal "circle, stand blindfolded by the point of a sword" kind of initiation, but rather of the "if it doesn't kill you, it will make you stronger" type. Traveling alone, waking up in different places, and the challenge of finding destinations you've never visited before, can all create a mind-bending experience. Like the lone tribesman on the top of a mountain or sequestered in a cave, such separation from the normal routines of life definitely can induce an altered state. I have a friend who travels regularly, taking road trips across the United States or backpacking across Europe, and when she came home and described these transcendental occurrences, I shook my head and thought, "It was just a vacation." Now I have a better idea of what she was talking about!

Tapped by a Mountain

Once of the most remarkable things on my initial trip was a visit to Mount Shasta. To start with, I didn't even realize I was going to the area. Following my trusty tour book's driving directions (this was in my pre-GPS days) I headed down Interstate 5 and then, as I crossed over from Oregon into Northern California, I was struck. That is the only way I have to explain it. It was as if I were asleep and someone tapped me on the shoulder to wake me up. In the distance, I saw a large mountain, surrounded by hills. In some strange way, they seemed related; it was like the mountains and hills were talking to each other. As they "spoke," they radiated a loving power that I could actually feel. Each mile I went, the field grew thicker and more energetically active, gradually feeling like warm water. I soon saw a sign and realized that the mountain was Mt. Shasta.

City Witchcraft

For those unfamiliar with this famous peak, many claim it as a holy site, perhaps one of the most magical places in North America. The mountain itself is sacred to the native peoples who settled the area, and it continues to attract people to this day. (I once had a teacher who was a bit "out there," and claimed that an advanced alien race lived beneath the mountain.)

While I was on the road, I got a very clear message that I needed a stone from the mountain. I was on an eight-hour road trip from one location to another, and I couldn't imagine stopping long enough to get to the mountain for an extended period of time to get a stone. I heard the voice in my head say, "You will get the stone, have no fear." My messages can be clear in deep meditation, but not usually when I'm driving! I'm not sure if the message was from the mountain spirit or my own guides, but it was loud and clear.

I stopped in Shasta City for lunch and found lots of crystal shops. I thought that perhaps one of these stores would have a stone from the mountain. As I inquired in each shop, they looked at me kind of strangely. Then, finally, the only shop that had any Witchcraft books had the stone I was looking for. They had a small supply of opals from the mountain itself. Before I even knew what they were, I was drawn to them, in the back corner of this tiny shop. I knew that my "Mt. Shasta guide" was right. I got my stone, and was able to continue on my journey roughly on schedule. I used the stone to connect to the energy of the mountain once I returned home.

Travel as Initiation

I can be a little dense when it comes to sensing energy; always before, when I visited other sacred places, I was disappointed that I didn't seem to feel what others were feeling.

Even at the fabled Sedona, Arizona, vortices I felt only a little "something," but I obviously wasn't bowled over like the rest of my tour group. So the experience of sensing the energy of Mt. Shasta was new to me. I wasn't even at the mountain, just on the road going by it. Still, I was overwhelmed. The sense of energy was so real, so palpable.

I believe the reason I was much more aware of this energy was the altered state I was already in — a state induced by my road trip. As my trip ended, I started to ponder the magick of cars. I had never through about the magical implications of the car itself before this trip but, upon reflection, our modern methods of travel are quite remarkable. I started to explore the concept of the car as our modern-day "chariot," and the associations the Chariot card has in Tarot, and the implications of both for the journey of our lives.

The Chariot card of the Tarot has many associations. My first Tarot teacher described it in the following way:

Imagine a triumphant soldier who has returned from a journey. Poised at the summit of possibility, he has to determine which path to take. Once the journey has begun and momentum is put behind the new path, it will be difficult to change. Contemplate your path, and then charge forward.

City Witchcraft

On a mundane level, the Chariot card often arises as an indication of travel difficulties or, conversely, opportunities. Pulling the Chariot card can mean car trouble, getting lost, or taking a trip. On the most esoteric level, the Chariot is the chariot of the gods, the shamanic vehicle known to the Jewish mystics as the Merkaba chariot. The ultimate journey is, of course, the shamanic journey, the journey of spirit to the other worlds. So the Chariot can also represent the journey of life, the driving representing the divine spirit.

With this in mind, I began, south of Shasta, to try to view my car as part of my magickal journey. In the following section are a few ideas of how you can work magickally with your car. One caveat: when doing any type of contemplations in your car, make sure safety comes first! Sometimes, it is possible to drive while in a light meditative state; however, use caution and common sense. If you are driving at night, in inclement weather, in heavy traffic, or otherwise need to be 100% alert, wait until you are a passenger before doing magick in your car!

Five Magical Car Trip Tips

1. Protect Your Car

One of the most basic spells of car magick is to use energy to protect your car. While in your car, imagine it surrounded by a crystal egg. Put into the "egg" your intention for protection from all harm. Imagine that the crystal allows energy into it that is needed, but blocks out all harm. Imagine it gently guiding you and sliding you into the right place, preventing all damage and accidents. Repeat the exercise as needed to reinforce your shield. This technique is especially good in rural places for keeping critters from running into the road in front of your car.

2. *Find a Parking Space*

The next most popular act of car magick is finding a parking space on a busy street or crowded lot. As you start your journey, take a moment to imagine your destination. Imagine a parking space right by the door and imagine yourself pulling into it. Don't imagine just an empty parking space. I've done that quite a bit, only to see someone else pull into "my" spot! Finally, I learned to visualize *my* car pulling into the space, and have had far greater success.

3. *Find Your Way*

Another much-needed spell is to receive guidance when driving. I've often found my way by opening up to my intuition and calling upon the "spirit of travelers." I think of the spirit as the god Hermes. Then I ask, "This way? Yes/No" or "right/left" and let the first answer that pops into my head by my guide. I think of my spirit guide as the true "driver" of my chariot, much like Krishna with Arjuna in the *Bhagavad Gita*. When the journey is done, I thank my guide. Note that spirit guides are no substitute for good directions, a map, and a GPS unit! Still, when you're having difficulties, be sure to use *all* your tools, including your intuition and spiritual guidance.

4. *Feel the Energy*

As you drive, open your intuition and allow information to come to you. Feel the various energy fields around you as you pass through different neighborhoods and locations. Like my visit to Mt. Shasta, let the energy pass through you. Recognize the different flavors and styles of energy. Allow the experience to inform you and see if there is anything you are drawn towards. Who knows what you might find along the road before you?

5. *Work Your Problems as You Drive*

As a part of dream magick, I learned a technique of focusing on your question, writing it out on a piece of paper, and then placing it under your pillow. As you sleep, lying in an altered state, your subconscious works on the problem and solves the issue for you. A similar technique is to write out a question or problem and place the paper beneath the driver's seat of your car. When your drive is done, take a moment to think about your situation and see if you have a fresh perspective. More often than not, the solution to my problem has presented itself after my drive.

Let your "chariot" be more than just a source of transportation. When we are truly living the magickal life, every action, no matter how mundane, is an opportunity to partner with the divine.

CHAPTER EIGHT: ENTERING THE URBAN GODS

Since walking the ways of the urban Witch in Boston many moons ago, it has been quite clear that each city and town has its own individual personality, both on a mundane level, and on the metaphysical. When communicating with the various spirits tied to urban locations, they seemed to reflect the overall vibe of the overarching city, as if they all belonged to a similar tribe. Time and again magickal people have shared with me their impressions about how they intuitively picked up on the personality of the city where they resided, often quite by accident, since few traditional magickal training books give instructions for such things. One friend recently commented on a city where he felt the spirit of the city merely tolerated his presence, but he wasn't welcome there, nor would he thrive. He just knew it walking the streets, even though his job was great, and culturally it had what he wanted in a city. His energy simply didn't resonate with the city, and the city let him know it. Luckily enough he was intuitively smart enough to get out.

Unfortunately the archetypes of the indwelling urban gods are not as clear as the images of our popular Pagan mythology. Though cities have archetypal forces inherent in them, few books, stories, or even visits spell them out as clearly and recognizably as the old myths. Few make their archetype and magickal qualities readily apparent. It takes a relationship with the city to draw out such personal information.

When on a trip to New Orleans, the magickal archetypes of the urban world became more apparent. Forces set my magickal mind in motion, to see things in a different light. I was speaking at "Saints & Sinners," a gay literature convention. While speaking on the spirituality panel, one gentleman kept referring to how New Orleans is truly a Scorpionic town. Everything is about sex and death, and many people have undergone great transformations while residing in the city. He then went out to demonstrate it, illustrating his point with a variety of authors and musicians. Sex, death and transformation are all key words associated with the archetype of Scorpio. If you visit the French Quarter on any evening, you can readily see how the air is permeated with sex and alcohol. Both can transform your view of the world. It was built on a swamp, fixed stagnant water, another symbol of Scorpio, on rotting wood, by the labor of slaves. Graves are built above ground due to the water table, so death is apparent all around, and the air of mystery, secrecy, danger and magick surrounded the locale if you looked for it. There is also a current of true spirituality there, again if you choose to look for it. I was lucky enough to find it amongst some practitioners who were looking beyond the tourist trade. I hadn't thought of it in terms of astrology, but New Orleans, or at least the French Quarter, fit the archetype of Scorpio exactly. Even my own experiences revolved around sexuality and transformation there, and were quite empowering.

New Orleans started my quest to look at urban spirits through the lens of astrology, but I was less successful than I had hoped. Though Scorpio is obviously an astrological sign, it also relates to the underworld deities of death and rebirth. Most cities, and spirits, are not always strongly defined by one of the twelve astrological archetypes. As people are a mix of all twelve signs, with different emphasis on different areas, so too are most other entities a complex blend. One only has to think about how many times the deities assignment to the signs has been juggled around with the changing attitudes of the society to that godform. There is not always an exact match. I tried looking to the founding dates of various cities, to cast astrological "birth" charts for them. I discovered that deciding which date to use what often hard, and exact "birth" times are not often listed. The discovery of a location, the founding of a colony, the technical founding of a city and its acceptance into a greater government or country could each pose as potential inception dates, yet none easily matched my experiences and expectations. I tried to gather information from mystical residents to see what sign each city corresponded to in their opinion. We flirted with New York City as Aquarian, being on the cutting edge of the global melting pot, yet that did not embody everything New York offers. We looked at Los Angeles as a Leo correspondent due to the plethora of show business, yet that didn't embody the spirit of the City of Angels in its entirety. They had some matching correspondences, but also some big gaps. So I was resigned to work back with techniques of personal experience and interpretation, rather than math and ephemeris tables.

My trip to New Orleans served as inspiration on a whole other level, in regards to urban gods and spirits. I was honored to be invited to a ritual that was a blend of Voodoo and other African Diaspora spirituality and took great interest in the similarities and differences between it and modern Witchcraft. Though I never had framed it in such a way before, I could see how such religions took the more nature-based principles and then, due to force, found a way to thrive in an urban environment. Methods of contacting their entities, the *Lwa*, were very visceral. When separated from the traditional offerings of Africa, new correspondences were found in the New World. Traditions evolved and adapted to the circumstances around them. These rich rituals and lore served as a modern magician's inspiration for working with the spirits dwelling within urban centers. Through it, I hopefully pass some inspiration on to you about contacting the urban gods.

Altar Building

The beautiful and complex altars found in Voodoo ceremonies and temples inspired me to look beyond the traditional Witch's tools when working in a modern context. Beyond the magickal workspace, altars can be focuses for building a relationship with a specific spirit, by devoting that space in your home to the spirit. Voodoo traditions have a wide variety of complex associations, including food, drinks and scents to evoke the spirit to whom the altar is dedicated.

For the spirits that embody the consciousness of a city, choose items that are "traditionally" linked to the city itself. States have particular flowers and birds dedicated to them that can be a starting point, but other items are more personal and representative of the city. Tourist gift shops are the best place to look. Is there a distinguishing landmark in your city – man made or natural? Does a particular building or museum automatically evoke thoughts of your city? A small replica of the Statue of Liberty suits a NYC altar. How about the corporate images of the local sports teams? Is your city known for a particular food or drink? Obviously foods that spoil quickly can only be a part of your altar for a short time, and can be a focus for a specific ritual, but you can include less perishable items associated with it. In an altar to build a relationship with the spirit of Boston, clam chowder would be a potential choice, but not one I would like to have sitting out for a period of time. But a small package of oyster crackers used in the chowder is a great addition to the altar.

If your location doesn't have such obvious correspondences, simple items directly from the city – leaves and stones from the city's park, coins found on its streets, subway or bus tokens, unpaid parking tickets, all can be found on the urban altar.

Sigils

I was fascinated with the drawings of the Voodoo *veves*, and how they appeared so much like an intricate sigil from a modern magician. Veves are symbols used to call the spirits. Each Lwa has its own veve associated with it. Lwa of love will often have heart imagery while those of the sea will have boat imagery. The veves are drawn out in powder upon the temple floor.

Veve of Legba

Urban practitioners can use meditation and intuition to create city sigils to embody the spirit of the city. My book *City Magick* has techniques for making city sigils in reference to specific intentions or spells, but these symbols can be more creative and primal, not for any one spell, but to evoke and connect with the god of the city. If the city is known by any distinguishing shapes or characteristics, they can be used as part of your personal connection to it. Boston is often referred to as "the Hub," so using the wheel-like or web-like imagery of the highways surrounding it is an excellent starting place. The outline of Manhattan and its grid system is another excellent base symbol. The bridges of San Francisco can be worked into their sigil, and double, or twin, imagery can be used for the twin cities of Minneapolis and St. Paul.

Evocation

One of the best teachings my music business professor in college gave me, regarding contract negotiation, was, "We don't get what we don't ask for." I carry those words with me in my magickal practice and spell craft. If we don't invest our time and our words into creating something in our life, then why should it happen? People will wish for something silently, but never really ask the universe for it outright, even when they have all the magickal skills to be successful. Life can be like a contract. If we don't negotiate and ask for what we want, we don't get it. We have to make sure we reflect and know that what we ask for is what we really want, on all levels. If you ask for it, you just might get it, and then be stuck with it!

Many mystics and Witches say they want to have a more magickal life, and see and communicate with the spirits in all things, but don't actively put any energy into it. Sometimes it is easier to complain. If you want to build a magickal relationship

City Witchcraft

with the spirit of your city, ask for it. Realize that this relationship is quite literally and figuratively a two way street, that the urban spirit will not only be able to help your life, but might ask you for help, being a force of stewardship and balance in the world. If that suits you, then perform an evocation. Build your altar. Draw your sigil. Then ask for it. Open your heart and call out to the spirit of the city. Offer your service, and ask for the type of relationship you want. Everybody's relationship with the city will be different. What are you offering, and what are you asking? Put your power in your words.

Pathworking

Pathworking, visualized meditation, journey work... whatever you choose to call it, it can be one of the most effective ways of building a relationship with a spirit. Through meditation or through lucid dreaming, get yourself into a deeper trance state, yet remain aware. Ask to visit with the spirit of the city, the indwelling urban god. Learn its lessons. Listen to its wisdom. See how it manifests and personifies, if at all, to you. Work with it directly, and it will reveal its own mysteries to you, beyond what any article, book or teacher can show you.

Like any other spirit or entity, always be respectful. It's hard for many to think of us as being reverent to urban entities, but at the very least treat these beings as you wish to be treated. Use your discernment. Such relationships tread new ground and are not necessarily for the inexperienced. Follow your heart, but also your mind and learn to flow with the tides of your own environment. As you find balance within yourself, you will help create balance in the city around you.

CHAPTER NINE: URBAN LOVE

Love is the heart of the best magick I've ever done. Magick is powered by our emotions, and although any strong emotion can fuel our spellcraft and kindle our will, I like focusing on the emotion of love whenever possible. If you believe that what you send out returns to you, then its great to power your spells through love, for it will manifest through love upon its return to you.

When people hear me talking about love and magick, some assume that it is a benign, airy, insubstantial love. Magickal love can be powerful, fierce and intense. In some traditions of Witchcraft, initiates are threatened by sword point, to only enter the magick circle in a state of Perfect Love and Perfect Trust. This spiritual love, unconditional love is not the personal love of movie and greeting cards, but a divine, all encompassing love.

Love comes in many forms. Our western culture and English language uses one word to describe many different states of consciousness. Love can involve friends, family, romantic partners, sexual passions, and spiritual devotion. Love represents a spectrum of awareness.

The urban world has many of us struggle with two currents in the spectrum of love – the romantic quest and the spiritual quest. Though seemingly unrelated, the lessons for both are quite magickal.

Spiritual Love

The quest for enlightenment does not seem particularly "urban," though for a Witch desiring to embody perfect love and perfect trust, it's an everyday struggle with the sheer number of people in one small space, from a variety of background, beliefs and personalities. Any major city is like a microcosm of the world. Multiple views are represented, and in this somewhat closed system, they all have to figure out not only how to get along, but how to eventually thrive for the betterment of all involved.

City living can be confrontational, to say the least, and the multitude of distractions assaulting our senses—pollution on the physical, visual, sonic and most importantly the psychic level—it is hard to find a state of peace and equilibrium, much less maintain it for very long in a provocative situation.

Many on the spiritual path equate spiritual, unconditional love, with unconditional relationships. They feel the model of love is complete receptivity and passivity. Such a path without both emotional and psychic boundaries is not very compatible with urban life, or in fact, with social community-based life, since defining our boundaries is an important aspect of maintaining our health and integrity.

Witches learn all about boundaries and, hopefully, can apply our magickal knowledge metaphorically in relationship as well. Casting ritual circle and creating sacred space creates boundaries, separating mundane times and activities from the spiritual, setting a "space beyond space and a time beyond time" to celebrate and make magick. The image used, a circle or energetic bubble, is a boundary, much like the sacred space around everybody's body, Witch and non-Witch alike, often referred to as our aura or energetic bodies. Most people perceive this as their "personal space," and know when someone has violated it by entering uninvited, or projecting a intimidating presence within it. We are sovereign in our personal space, unless we cannot maintain the boundaries of it and allow uninvited guests, and uninvited psychic energy into it, like legends about inviting a vampire into one's home.

My perceiving the aura as a personal temple of perfect love and perfect trust, a sacred magick circle, around us all the time, we can use our magick to create greater health and well being in our daily life. Such thoughts do not mean we are constantly "between the worlds" and ungrounded throughout our daily life. We can be in sacred space and still grounded in the physical world. It takes the attitude of seeing the sacred in all places, all people, and all situations. That's a tough job. We don't want to see the sacred when people upset us, make us angry, sad, or tired. But it is in those situations when it is the most important of all to see the sacred in everyone.

Perfect love, or unconditional love, is seeing the sacred in all things, but it is impersonal. The love is not a response of personally liking or not liking someone. It is based on their innate, divine nature. It is detached from the personal. You can have unconditional love without unconditional relationships by knowing the difference between the two levels of being.

Personally, I can think you are a big jerk who is trying to hurt my feelings and be very angry with you but, simultaneously, I can love the divine essence within you. That second current helps me respond appropriately to the situation, rather than react and say or do something I might regret. But even with that second, impersonal, perspective, I might decide that appropriate thing is to express my righteous anger of the situation, and let you know your behavior is wholly inappropriate. I don't love you any less on the divine level, and that frames my response in a manner aligned with higher guidance.

People think that if they love someone unconditionally, they should let that person say or do anything they want, because any other action would mean they were not a spiritually "loving" person. That is simply untrue! They are confusing the personal boundary with the detached, impersonal perspective. If you love yourself unconditionally, which is the requisite for loving another, you have to love yourself enough to maintain your own health and sanity.

I can feel a great love for you, but not even really know you personally. Often at healing workshops that generate a great sense of unconditional love, people walk away feeling incredibly connected. They maintain contact, and then later feel shocked by the person they get to know. Some feel betrayed because the personal contact did not live up to the intense, unconditional love of a magickal retreat. The friend did not betray you, you simply got to know them on the personal love, and they turned out to be different than your ideal of them. Until we study forms of mysticism, we are not taught the differences between these kinds of love – personal and unconditional.

Personal Sacred Space

Maintaining dual perspectives of personal and impersonal worlds is very difficult. It is one of the ways Witches can exist "between the worlds" yet be fully in the physical and grounded. I find it quite helpful in the most exasperating situations, though it's not foolproof. We all have moments when we confuse the two. It's part of the human experience and completely natural and normal. The more we can maintain balance, and express ourselves in a healthy way, the greater chance we can create our community with a harmony for all.

Try this exercise to help maintain your personal sacred space between these two perspectives. It will maintain boundaries between yourself and the energies that might overwhelm you in the world.

Sit quietly in a meditative state. Imagine the space around you as a bubble or vortex of energy. I imagine myself in an egg like shape of colored light. The light on the inside shell of the "egg" is like a churning liquid that moves and responds to my thoughts and emotions. Imagine at the bottom of this shape is a deep tap root, an energetic tail that grounds you, like a grounding wire, tied deep in the earth.

Using your will, focus the energy of your eggshell, making it crystalize, giving it a quartz like quality, making it semi transparent. With this crystal shield, you are programming it to allow in whatever you need, but to block out what you don't. Surround your shield with a "transformative" fire and light. I imagine it as a violet or purple flame, but whatever colors symbolize transformation to you.

Allow whatever unwanted energies coming your way to "burn" in the transformative flame, and direct the ash down to the bottom of the shell, down through the tap root, where the Earth can transform it.

When you feel yourself in a reactive mode, when your emotional state gets personal and uncomfortable, and you feel unable to see the divinity in a situation (and we all do no matter how advanced we might think we are) mentally activate the flame. Feel it dissolve away the unhealthy links and cords we form, and even dissolve away our own unhealthy feelings we could be projecting. Allow the shield and flame to help you detach from the immediacy of the situation, and view it from another perspective. It doesn't mean your problem or issue will magically go away. It doesn't mean people will always say nice things, or even what you want to hear. It will create some breathing room so you can reflect and explore your feelings, rather than blindly reacting to the situation.

Romantic Love

Only once we have a strong sense of self-identity and personal boundaries are we ready for a serious romantic relationship. There's something about the magick of cities that naturally calls romantics together. Kindred souls, seeking the arts, education, excitement, and any of the other attractions of the city life, find joy in each other's arms, and true understanding of their interests and passions.

Cities inspire the feeling of magick, that you can find that true special someone. I know when I was dating, some of the most magickal romantic moments were set amid the picturesque scenes of Boston, Cambridge, and trips to New York City. The lights and skyline, the vibrant artistic scene and the plethora of exciting restaurants and shops to explore together make an adventure for any new couple. Walking the streets of Montreal with my partner, we were reminded of the magick of our first few dates, sitting out by the sidewalk cafés, talking for hours. Cities inspire people to find their hearts and come together in love.

Unfortunately, many seek out excitement and romance as a distraction from learning self-love and self-identity. Many have the erroneous notion of "finding their other half" or being otherwise incomplete, and needing the love of another to fulfill and "complete" them. Those are the ones who often feel betrayed by the mystery and magick of the city, continually finding their "soul" mate, a new one each week or month, and continually disappointed that their "ideal" partner did not turn out the way they expected. From the magickal perspective, such notions confuse the personal and impersonal spheres and create disillusionment and heartbreak.

The key to breaking the cycle is a strong sense of self and an understanding that you are a reflection of the universe. Everybody is. You are complete unto yourself. Everybody is. No one is needed for completion or perfection, regardless of what romantic notions or New Age doctrine you might have. A romantic partner (or partners for those seeking polyamorous relationships) are ideally compliments to you, and you to them. But you are solely responsible for your own health, happiness and well being. It's no one's job to take care of all your needs. No one magically fits your every want and desire.

Relationships are work. Our storybook romances, particularly our books and movies set amid the romantic urban backdrop, end with the first union, be it kiss, date, or wedding, and then the assumed "happily ever after" but such unions are only the beginning of relationship. All the work of a relationship is not idealized, so it doesn't make it to the silver screen.

Love Magick

Though in the first half of this article we used sacred space to maintain boundary and balance between our personal and impersonal perspectives, we can use our sacred space, and the flowing currents of energy interwoven in the cities, to attract those who are correct and good for us as romantic partners. If you feel you have a strong sense of self and are ready for such work, try this ritual.

Get your favorite sweet treat from someplace in the city—pastries or sweet bread work wonderfully. Make sure it's something soft, and not a hard candy. Cleanse two copper pennies, the metal of Venus, in running water. Your tap water is fine. Ideally on a Friday evening, when the Moon is waxing, think about your ideal lover. Call upon the deities of love. In this modern era we commonly think of Venus/Aphrodite and Eros, but use whatever pantheon you feel the strongest connection. Hold the two pennies and think about the qualities you wish to attract and the type of relationship you desire. I personally suggest not focusing on an individual you know, but the type of lover you desire, leaving the right one to come to you. I also would put in a catch phrase such as "I ask this be for the highest good, harming none" just to make sure things don't backfire. Take a small bite of your treat, to taste the sweetness you wish in your love life. Place the two pennies into the pastry and then take a journey to a location in the city where you reside that is romantic to you. You destination can be near a particularly romantic restaurant, a happening nightclub scene, or anyplace else that resonates with the type of love you want. Leave the penny laced treat in a crossroads near the romantic spot, allowing the energy of the crossroads, a place in between place, to guide your new love to your life. Then be open and aware, yet not obsessive, of new possibilities for you.

Explore the many types of love and love magick. Hold love within your heart and send it out around you. Your efforts will be rewarded on the personal, romantic, and spiritual levels.

CHAPTER TEN: PENNIES FROM HEAVEN

Money. Can't live in the big city without it. Everything costs something. Nobody rides for free. If you want to live in the urban landscape—and live *comfortably*—you need some coin of the realm to get you by. Unfortunately, most people spend all their waking time struggling in jobs that will pay more and more, yet spend their lives unfulfilled. Many people think they work to live, and enjoy their evenings and weeknights, even if they have to suffer forty hours plus a week. And some do. I have quite a few friends who live by the motto "work hard, play hard," even if they are working hard at something they don't like.

When I was at BEA, the Book Expo America, in Chicago I met some amazing people and had a great time, but one meeting in particular stood out. I was speaking with a small publisher of Eastern spirituality books. One of their newest titles was about finding peace and serenity in your day job. As I spoke to the salesman, just doing the obligatory convention floor chat, he was so enthused about its potential for sales. "Everybody hates their job, don't they?" he said to me. He was winding up for a sales pitch, assuming I was some type of retailer. "I don't," I replied. He told me he did, even though it was the best job he had ever had. He really wanted to open his own business, but was afraid it wouldn't make enough money, so he decided to work for another publisher. He wasn't even into Eastern spirituality personally.

I was a little shocked at this spiritual publisher pushing people to settle for something that isn't rewarding, but to find the bliss in it anyway. On one hand I can understand. It's the old eastern secret to life. Chop wood. Carry water. What do you do once you reach enlightenment? You still chop wood and carry water, but now you see the spirit in every moment, and mundane tasks take on a deeper significance. You can find divine bliss in the most mundane of experiences, because everything is ultimately spiritual. Okay, we've all had our "wood and water" jobs on the career path. And we will always have our wood and water chores. Mine is more like do laundry, take out the trash. Although we might always be a part of daily work, a daily grind, we don't have to be slaves to it. But still, isn't there something more?

The answer is in our relationship, not only with prosperity, but our relationship with our will. When we perform magick, for the sake of simplicity, we organize it with categories. We have healing magick. We try our hand at love magick. And most important to so many people who cross my doorstep, we seek our fortunes through money magick. In the end, all of these magickal forms are fueled by our will. Not only do we explore our personal will, what we want here and now, in the moment and hopefully with some forethought, but what our magickal self wants, what our higher will, or what some magicians call the True Will, wants. The best magick supports our True Will, our purpose or calling in the world, and very often our True Will is interwoven with our life's vocation, whatever it may be. Practitioners of the western magickal paths, from ceremonial magick to Witchcraft, don't just seek to find the spiritual in the mundane, though it's hopefully a by-product of our quest, we seek to fulfill our True Will, making every action we take a sacred step in fulfilling our will in the world.

Before we delve into the world of True Will, let's look at our traditional solutions to money woes. In the mundane world, people often pick their job based on what pays the best, and do not always factor in things like "Where will I be happiest?" "What is the community like?" "Am I really called to do this job?" Money is a factor, but not always the most important factor. I've found people who picked really fun jobs that paid less than what their experience and training was worth, but it worked out for everybody in the end. They lived a more fulfilled, happy, and prosperous life.

In the magickal world, most people wait to the crisis point and try working a quick cash spell. We've all done it, myself included. I've bathed myself in fast money oil. When you have an immediate need, like rent, or something you want to get before the sale ends, desperation can breed magickal miracles. Suddenly you get a check, gift, or series of payments that matches the amount you need, rarely more or less.

The second phase of money magick for most practitioners is abundance. People want abundance. They do a lot of work for abundance—affirmations, prayers, spells—but they never specify what *kind* of abundance they want. I'm reminded of lessons by wonderful wise woman and author Dorothy Morrison. Abundance just means a lot of something. You can have an abundance of gold, or an abundance of misfortune. You need to specify. The universal powers will simply fulfill your spell in the easiest manner possible, and not fulfill what you *think* you wanted. If you want an abundance of cash, you have to work that intention clearly into your magick. Don't assume the universe knows what you "really" meant. Your intention must be crystal clear.

I think true money magick comes in the relationship to prosperity. To be prosperous refers to both economic success and, in general, healthy growth. To be prosperous means you flourish, having everything you need to be successful. Like a healthy plant in a garden, you have all the soil, minerals, light, and water you need to grow. Prosperity magick is not always about dollar signs, but about having everything you want and need. I may not be a rich person by traditional worldly reckoning, but I am a very prosperous person.

Becoming a truly prosperous person usually requires some deep introspection. In Witchcraft, we face our fears, or shadows, the energies that self-sabotage. I have found a big aspect of shadow work is exploring any blocks you have towards prosperity. You would think we would all be perfectly open to creating prosperity, but due to our beliefs, upbringing and deep seated thoughtforms, we aren't. Many people lack self worth and on some deep level don't feel they deserve prosperity and success. Some followed parental models that instilled the belief you cannot like your job, but you have to do it. I'm always surprised to find people who feel guilty for getting paid for something they enjoy doing. Those in the arts—from music, graphics, and performance—to the spiritual and healing arts, often struggle with the mistaken belief they shouldn't be paid for their creativity. They want to share their gifts, and feel so much enjoyment from doing their arts, they feel guilty when financially compensated. I know I've struggled with that belief myself as an artist, musician, and psychic reader. In the end, to be prosperous you have to realize your time, skills, and effort are as valuable, in their own way, as a doctor, lawyer, executive or investor.

We have religious and societal associations that make us feel bad about wanting money, luxury, and prosperity. Many spiritual seekers throughout the ages take vows of poverty to devote themselves selflessly to their spiritual work. I find it interesting that the teachers and institutions that often promote these beliefs, from the Catholic Church to popular gurus, all seem to live more than comfortably and have the resources for whatever they want. I was lucky that when I started in the Craft, my first teachers emphasized that our path is about balance. We don't seek riches or poverty in and of themselves. We seek balance and the resources to do our work in the world. When we are comfortable and taken care of in our needs, we can do work to help others and the world. Without using the words, they were really teaching principles similar to Maslow's Hierarchy of Needs. They taught me money is simply an energy, to be stored, saved, and expended as you desire. There is nothing immoral or wrong with it. It is neutral, like magickal energy. The morals depend on how you use it.

Maslow's Hierarchy of Needs

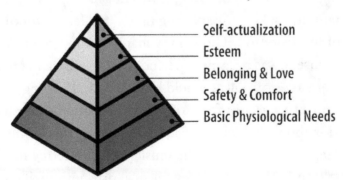

- Self-actualization
- Esteem
- Belonging & Love
- Safety & Comfort
- Basic Physiological Needs

Though we live in a society of traditional economics, supply and demand with a finite set of resources, magickal views on prosperity give us an ever abundant view of life when we are aligned with our magickal will. Your will does not directly conflict with the True Will of anyone else. All the resources you need will be at your command. You can have a win-win situation, where in this spiritual model, if you get the job or resources you want, you are not taking it away from someone else, but following your True Will. If they did not get it, then their will is found elsewhere. I know it sounds like a certain amount of new age gobbledegook, but from personally being on the losing side of the equation more than once, I can attest that each loss brought me closer into understanding my true purpose, at least at that point in time. It's a constant quest to be "on purpose" in everything, and we can experience it for a time, and then slide off for a bit, feeling lost, only to find a new purpose and direction for our will.

When I began my adventures in the working world, I was seeking fame and fortune. I wanted to be a rock star. I had just started on my path as a Witch, and used my magick to find the members of my band, book gigs, create semi-successful recordings. As you can imagine, it was not my True Will to be a world-famous rock star. Exploring music and learning skills was a part of my True Will. Though my magick supported it for a time because it was a learning period. It was a fun and effective way to gain a set of skills I would later need in the long term. I learned how to speak in front of people, negotiate contracts, do promotion, book events, and tour. I needed all these skills in my writing career. But once the music was distracting me from the next step in the path, all my musical prosperity fell out from under me. I lost my band. I lost my job in the industry. I lost interest in music and found myself, through spiritual guidance, gravitating towards writing and teaching. When my ego desires conflicted with the next step of my True Will, my magick no longer worked. My prosperity dried up when I was not "on purpose" and once I got back onto the path of my True Will, many new opportunities were made available. The trick is balancing your will, your efforts – magickal and mundane – with listening to your guidance, to hear the voice of your True Will. Magick is both doing and listening, ritual and meditation or divination, though sometimes it's more effective to listen first, and get some guidance before setting forth on a given path.

Penny Spell

While visiting a new city where I was booked for a day of tarot readings and a book signing, the city itself inspired this bit of prosperity magick. I was told by the store owner that no one had signed up for my tarot readings, though I was counting on a fairly prosperous day to help fuel the rest of my trip. As I was walking around, I kept finding pennies. Whenever I find change, I always pick it up and think about it as a sign, a blessing of prosperity from the gods. I accept little gifts and big gifts, as they come my way. This time it wasn't just one or two, or even three, but by the end of my walk, I had collected eleven.

As I picked up the pennies, I thought of the reciprocal nature of prosperity, to give as well as to receive. Beside doing the more substantial charitable donations to local groups, I give away my pocket change to those who ask for it, from those on the street to charitable organizations that fit with my own beliefs and practices. I wondered about why I was finding all these pennies and if it meant anything. Then I was struck to "give" the pennies back to the spirit of the city, as an offering, to ask for a blessing. I added one penny to the pile, making twelve in all. I took another walk, and in twelve strategic places, wherever my intuition led me, I put down a penny heads up. I wasn't sure why, but when I was done, I felt like I had accomplished something.

The next day, I went to the metaphysical store to fulfill my tarot time, even with no clients lined up, just in case there was a walk in. I was shocked to get enough walk ins to fill the twelve half hour readings slots of the day. I was flabbergasted. Though laying out the pennies was not a specific act of magick with a clear intention, it was an act of reciprocity, of giving back to the spirits of the place and asking for their blessing. I showed up to do the work I was contracted for, and even though it appeared I wasn't going to get paid for my time, I was compensated quite well for the work I was willing to do. When we keep the principles of prosperity in our daily lives, we live prosperous lives. The next time you receive a boon in life, think of how you can pass it on, how you can share the blessings, ritually or

City Witchcraft

practically. Through this exchange you keep the wheel of life turning and move on-track to fulfilling your own will in the world.

CHAPTER ELEVEN: THE URBAN WEB

When I look at the city from above, in a tall building, from a plane or simply on a map, I am always struck by how much of a web the interconnected pathways form. I see a web in the merging of streets. Even many of the more orderly grid systems, like NYC, have areas where the regimented order breaks down. Still, there is pattern, and beauty in that pattern. The city is a mass of many webs and grids. Besides the streets and roads, the wires, lines, and pipes connecting electric, communication and utility systems are web-like, and stretch out into the suburbs and beyond. We have literally created a "worldwide web" of wires. Such webs are alluded to in some native prophecies, but it remains to be seen if this work will helps us, like the spinning spider, or be our doom, like the trapped fly.

I'm fascinated with the web imagery because I have a spiritual connection to the spirit of Spider. Spider has been a great teacher, through both difficulties and ease. I look for my lessons in spider imagery. Past history has shown me it's better for me to find them before they find me. So I wondered what this urban spider thinking meant for me. Unlike a lot of other insect and animal totems, spiders are found in the homes and offices of the urban dweller. But I knew it was more than that.

Spider Teachings

I started to reflect on the lessons of Spider. My first spidery lesson was about fear, learning to understand and accept that which is different from me. I can see such a lesson played out in the urban environment, where many different cultures and people mingle.

Its web is a symbol of patience. The spider spins it with intention, creating both home and a means to eat, but must

City Witchcraft

wait for it to manifest. The spider cannot make the prey come. The spider must create with intention, but detachment. The feast could be any number of insects. When living and working in the city, and now having some perspective having a lot of time out of that environment, I notice that many people, much like the spider, go through routines of frenzy activity punctuated by period of waiting, of feeling somewhat stuck. They live in a state of feast or famine. Some literally do so, particularly in the case of those involved in the arts and music. Most do so spiritually and energetically, stuck in a rut waiting until something enters their "web" their personal space and get things going and a new goal is set.

The web is a sign of communication. Myths say the first letters were written in the spider's web. The city is overflowing with written communication. Street and traffic signs are everywhere, guiding those seeking out new paths. Written advertisements, billboards, and shops signs entice passers-by. Don't forget the artistic, social, and political expressions found in graffiti. The letters and messages of the modern world are written in the urban web.

The most important teaching of Spider, and the web, is interconnection of all life, and in fact, all things. The web is often considered the symbol of all life, as the web of life is the chain of energies, physical and subtle, that link us all. When one moves upon this web, the vibrations are felt throughout it, though most humans are not attuned to these subtle shifts in perception, but must learn to be to find balance and harmony in the coming age.

Interconnection

This interconnection is the particularly important lesson for the city Witch or mage, as the metropolitan experience is a microcosm for the world, with many lands and cultures represented in a small space. Many city walkers, magickal and mundane, have the duel characteristics of both being able to rigidly block out a lot of energies and distractions that can be overwhelming to those of us with more delicate system while at the same time carry an intuitive knowing of the vibrations across the web. They take advantage of synchronicities and awareness that many others will miss. They have a hidden connection to their community and comrades, to find potential advantages and even simple good times, while learning to avoid pitfalls and dangers.

These occurrences seem to occur with more frequency in the urban environment than the suburbs or country dwelling. I work in the small town in which I was raised. I shop, dine, and do many errands there, but very rarely do I see anybody I know from my past. But I can find myself in Boston or Manhattan, and more often than not, randomly run into long lost friends without warning.

Though the city is vast, it creates certain strands of the web where those of similar intent and vibration can gather together —be it a specific neighborhood district, shopping area or local scene. Like the Law of Sympathy says, "like attracts like" and those of a similar vibration find themselves together. City dwellers create community webs within the city and stretching beyond as we become a more global society. From these strands we have the folk wisdom of the "six degrees of separation." When you add friends, companions, and acquaintances from the Internet, the reach of your community web becomes truly vast.

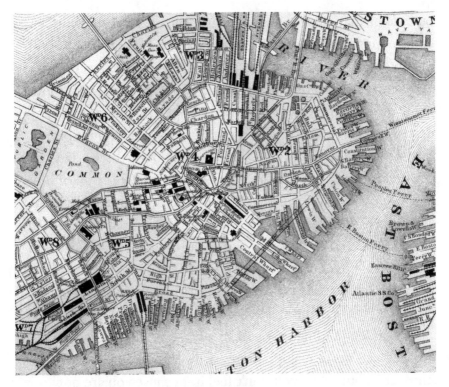

The "Web" of Boston

The Weaver

So for the city Witch, what does this spider philosophy have to do with magick and spiritual development? I'm always challenging myself to see things in new ways, and use traditional wisdom as a foundation, but take it to new places for myself. One of the major complaints many aspiring Witches have about the urban world is feeling disconnected. They feel isolated from the source of their magickal power, nature. They do not feel a part of the vast web of life because traditional lore uses the images of the bare earth, grass, trees, and running water to create that connection. They are all wonderful ways to connect with life, and in some ways preferable. But again, when we are outside of that environment, we are still a part of the world, and we must find ways to connect.

To some, the Goddess, in a vast and beautiful aspect, is the Weaver. I think of our image of the triple goddess, with roots in many different myths, as the Weaver. She creates, sustains, and destroys. The image of the Fates or Norns, where one spins, one measures, and one cuts the thread of our lives, as they are woven together into the tapestry of the world. I see all of life as a woven creation of this vast goddess. In my visions, I see the Goddess with three faces but, in a Hindu inspired image, many armed. As three are one, she has six arms, and two legs, making eight limbs, much like a spider goddess, weaving the world with her web. By focusing on your connection to her web, you are connected to her, and to all of creation.

By understanding that you are always a part of the web of life, you can make magick more easily. Intellectually you can know this, but when you don't feel it, because you are not connected to the web through nature, your magick can feel ineffectual. When you contemplate the web in a new, expanded way – including urban images, you feel a part of the network once again. Contemplate the web, including phone lines and streets, and internet connections and your circle of friends reaching out across the world.

Much of our modern magick is not lightning bolts from the sky and fire from our fingertips. Though at times I admit it would be nice, that is the magick of movies and myths. Our real magick manifests through synchronicities. They seem like coincidences to many but, with repeated success, you realize that magick, not luck, is at work. Magick takes the easiest route to manifest. We focus on the end result, but like the spider, are detached from how we get what we want, detached from what package it shows up in. Fly, moth, or butterfly? Doesn't matter as long as we eat. But we have to spin the web. We have to give the magick the opportunity to manifest through some channel. We cannot do a new job spell and then stay home and refuse to take calls or see people. If we network, interview, and search, through our magick we can find exactly the kind of job we desire, but we have to wait in the web, not hind in our hole (unless you're a trap-door spider...).

When you think of your interconnected web of friends, co-workers, and acquaintances, and how there have already been synchronicities from seemingly chance meetings, you understand that you have many channels through which your magick can manifest. You are already part of the vast web. Your own web is interconnected with many other people. You just have to weave your magick with intention, and let the desire manifest. Magick often works through a shifting of resources. What is nectar to you is poison to another, so as one person in your web discards something, if it is something you need and want, the message will come to you. One person can leave a job they hate because it is ill-suited for that person. But it might be perfect for you, and hearing about it through your network will give you the advantage to seek it out. The more you live with intention, the more you will manifest a magickal life.

Ritual of the Web

This ritual meditation is designed to help you align to the powerful forces already in your life. As you open to the urban web around you, you will find yourself more centered and secure and more magically alive. You will know the power to manifest your dreams exists all around you, no matter where you are.

Materials Needed:
  Flat Surface: A tray with no pattern on it works well,
     particularly if you cannot clear the surface of your altar.
  Salt or Cornmeal
  8 Items that represent areas of your life
  1 Item that represents you
  3 Candles, any colors you desire.

Start the ritual by clearing yourself and your space, getting centered and purified. Create sacred space in whatever way suits you. Clear your surface working space. Light your three candles, one for each aspect of the goddess. Collectively think of her as the weaver. If you have any other candles you would like to light, or incense, do so now. Put on any meditative ritual music you prefer.

In the center of your working surface, put the object that symbolizes you and your life. I like to use my pentacle ring, but you can use a photograph, stone, tarot card, or anything you'd like. At the edge of the working surface, moving clockwise, put the eight symbols of the various aspects of your life. They can be a combination of social groups and locations. For example, you can use a business card for your work life, a family antique for home, a photo of your friends, a printed email from your online correspondence, a matchbook from your favorite bar, a take out menu from a neighborhood restaurant , a theater playbill or movie ticket, and a leaf from a tree in the local park.

Take your bowl of salt or corn meal and focus your attention on it. I prefer to do this in salt, as salt is a great conductor of energy. Some traditions only use salt for protection, binding, and neutralization spells, so if you feel that is the only use of salt in magick, then you can use corn meal, flour, or even sand.

City Witchcraft

Use the central symbol for you as the hub, and create eight spokes with your powdered substance, like the strands of a web coming out from the center, to each of your eight objects. You are weaving a web, and through it, creating a magickal mandala. Feel how all these areas of life are connected to you, as the central point. Then, starting in the center, create a clockwise spiral of powder, connecting each of the spokes over and over again, like a spider weaving the web. Realize this spiral goes out infinitely, connecting you to realms beyond.

Focus on the mandala of your life you have created. Close your eyes and contemplate on the weaver's web. Feel yourself as both a part of creation and a weaver yourself. When you are done, return to normal consciousness and ground yourself.

In future versions of this ritual, if you want to create a change or manifest something in your life, replace one of the eight spots with a symbol of what you want to manifest. When you contemplate the mandala, imagine yourself in the center of the web, pulling toward you what you want to create, affirming or breaking lines of connection to things in your life. Know that you are a part of the act of creation. Know that magick is all around you, in every environment. Feel your magick in the center of the web.

Special thanks to my friend Christopher Giroux for adding to my insight and understanding of Spider.

ABOUT THE AUTHOR

Christopher Penczak is a teacher and co-founder of the Temple of Witchcraft and the author of numerous books, including the *Three Rays of Witchcraft, Plant Spirit Familiar, The Gates of Witchcraft, Feast of the Morrighan,* and *Buddha, Christ, Merlin. City Magick,* the inspiration for this title, was his first published book. Visit his website at *www.christopherpenczak.com.*

The Temple of Witchcraft
MYSTERY SCHOOL AND SEMINARY

Witchcraft is a tradition of experience, and the best way to experience the path of the Witch is to actively train in its magickal and spiritual lessons. The Temple of Witchcraft provides a complete system of training and tradition, with four degrees found in the Mystery School for personal and magickal development and a fifth degree in the Seminary for the training of High Priestesses and High Priests interested in serving the gods, spirits, and community as ministers. Teachings are divided by degree into the Oracular, Fertility, Ecstatic, Gnostic, and Resurrection Mysteries. Training emphasizes the ability to look within, awaken your own gifts and abilities, and perform both lesser and greater magicks for your own evolution and the betterment of the world around you. The Temple of Witchcraft offers both in-person and online courses with direct teaching and mentorship. Classes use the *Temple of Witchcraft* series of books and CD Companions as primary texts, supplemented monthly with information from the Temple's Book of Shadows, MP3 recordings of lectures and meditations from our founders, social support through group discussion with classmates, and direct individual feedback from a mentor.

For more information and current schedules, please visit: *www.templeofwitchcraft.org*.

CPSIA information can be obtained
at www.ICGtesting.com
Printed in the USA
JSHW031211190322
23961JS00007B/234